UN CHIEN

LUIS BUÑUEL AND
SALVADOR DALI

foreword by Jean Vigo

transcription and introduction by
Phillip Drummond

faber and faber
LONDON · BOSTON

First published in 1994
by Faber and Faber Limited
3 Queen Square London WC1N 3AU

Photoset in Plantin by Parker Typesetting Service, Leicester
Printed in England by Clays Ltd, St Ives, plc

Original shooting script © *L'Avant-Scène du Cinéma* and Luis Buñuel, 1963
English translation © Lorrimer Publishing Ltd, 1968
Introduction and transcription © Phillip Drummond, 1994
Photographs courtesy of BFI Stills, Posters and Design
Photograph on page 2 © the Buñuel family

A CIP record for this book is available
from the British Library

ISBN 0 571 17372 1

2 4 6 8 10 9 7 5 3 1

Contents

Philip Drummond has been Director of the MA Media Programme at the University of London Institute of Education since 1980. He is Media Coordinator for Network Educational Science Amsterdam. A former Co-Director of the International Television Studies Conference, his publications include *National Identity and Europe: The Television Revolution* (co-ed., London: British Film Institute, 1993). For a more detailed analysis of *Un Chien Andalou*, see his article 'Textual Space in *Un Chien Andalou*' (*Screen*, vol. 18, no. 3, Autumn 1977, pp. 55–119).

Surrealism and *Un Chien Andalou*

Introduction

The interaction between Surrealism and the cinema has been rich and varied. It involved, initially, a small group of films produced within the framework of the French Surrealist movement of the 1920s, among which *Un Chien Andalou* (*An Andalusian Dog*, 1929) stands as the brief, comic, terrifying landmark. The Buñuel/Dali film is flanked by such key works as Dulac's *The Seashell and the Clergyman* (1927), Cocteau's *The Blood of a Poet* and Buñuel's *L'Age d'Or* (both 1930). The broader membership of the canon is a matter of debate, but if we expand the historical frame it also designates a wider range of films and aspirations which emerge persistently through the subsequent half-century and offer their own versions of that original adventure, in all its magnificent and incoherent eccentricity. Works as diverse as the films of Lynch or Svankmajer, certain strands of film and television comedy and much of the output of the modern advertising industry are heirs apparent to that earlier convulsion in the artistic and cinematic imagination.

Their textual differences apart, Surrealist films share a range of common interests which are partly to do with the reality to which they refer, and partly with their vision of the cinema itself. They prefer to locate the real beyond the surface of immediate visibility, in hidden or repressed dimensions of society and of the psyche. The unconscious, and the dream, are key sites for these adventures. They are committed to exploring psychological and generally subjective states, and are drawn to the dramatic themes of sexuality and eroticism, especially as they connect to forms of violence. In addition, they tend to take a critical approach to a society which has papered over these realities, unable to address them without self-censorship.

Surrealist cinema draws its inspiration less from the dominant conventions of the Hollywood text than from the free-form impetus of other expressive media, most notably poetry and painting in the era of high Modernism. Classic cinema, however, remains valuable for Surrealism thanks to its stress on notions of adventure, psychological and physical, and for the lyricism of its comic vision. The semiotics of the dream – the Freudian structures of condensation and displacement – provide important inspirations. Surrealist films are thus constructed according to new approaches – sometimes playful, sometimes extremely earnest – to the conventions of cinematic language, usually venturing well beyond the customary boundaries of realism and narrative.

As Buñuel's biographer Francisco Aranda reminds us, few if any commercial films – and, one might add, few short films at that – have had such a 'triumphal' career as *Un Chien Andalou*, or have attracted such a volume and variety of critical attention. The film has been invoked, after all, as the point of generic intersection between film and poetry, as the fountain-head for Surrealism in the commercial cinema, and as the root source of cinematic modernism in general. This accumulation of criteria and accolades runs the risk, however, of reducing the text to the mere panache of its arrival. Too often it leaves the film either unread or misunderstood because of critical inflation or reduction. What is needed is a different and more detailed understanding of how the film came to be produced, and how it makes meaning. The mystery of *Un Chien Andalou* begins, in fact, with confusions concerning its conception and production. The incompleteness of available data and the competitive and mutually contradictory reminiscences of Buñuel and Dali impede definitive description, but the known facts and held opinions may be summarized as follows.

Buñuel and Dali: From Spain to France

In the later 1920s Buñuel and Dali emigrated from Spain to France to develop their incipient careers. Dali did not move permanently to Paris until the production period of *Un Chien Andalou* in early 1929, at the age of 24; for Buñuel, four years his senior, the film crystallized an involvement with the French avant-garde dating back to his arrival from Madrid in early 1925, a few months after the publication of the First Surrealist Manifesto in 1924. He had obtained a notional job supporting the Spanish representative in the planned 'International Institute of Intellectual Cooperation' being formed under the aegis of the League of Nations. In the meantime, Buñuel's mother paid for his ticket and gave him an allowance; four years on, she was to become the unwitting sponsor of what was to be one of the most celebrated and shocking short films in the history of the cinema. Buñuel's youthful interest in puppetry, his experience of amateur theatricals at the University of Madrid and his short 1926 play *Hamlet* led to an early breakthrough when he was offered the job as scenic director on Manuel de Falla's puppet opera, *El Retablo de Maese Pedro*. This short work, based on an episode from *Don Quixote*, was performed in Amsterdam in late April 1926.

From Theatre to Cinema

Buñuel's scenographic interests – apparently confirmed by an encounter with Fritz Lang's *Destiny* – led him to an informal apprenticeship with the French director Jean Epstein. He joined the latter's acting school and assisted on two productions – *Mauprat* (1926), in which he also appeared as an extra, and *The Fall of the House of Usher* (1928). In addition to his work for Epstein, Buñuel had a bit part in Jacques Feyder's *Carmen – Espagne Oblige* (1926) and worked on the Nalpas/Etiévant film *The Siren of the Tropics* (1927), starring Josephine Baker. The film was to introduce Buñuel to the talents of Pierre Batcheff and Albert Duverger, both subsequently recruited for *Un Chien Andalou*. Involvement in theatrical and film production meshed with Buñuel's work as a film critic and as a programme organizer. In Paris, he acted as film editor for the Spanish magazine *La Gaceta Literaria Hispanoamericana* and a critic for the Parisian journal *Les Cahiers d'Art*, seeing up to three films per day. In the Spanish magazine in 1927 he published Dali's article 'Artistic Film, Anti-artistic Film'. His relationship with the Parisian journal was short-lived, terminating in early 1928 over a dispute concerning Buñuel's abiding passion for American cinema.

Buñuel's writings for these and other publications fall into three related categories. There are, predominantly, reviews of individual films or film-programmes – *Greed, Metropolis, Joan of Arc, Camille, Napoleon, Rien que les Heures, College, The Way of All Flesh*. Buñuel also debates the merits of the purely visual continuity of avant-garde work versus the literary armature of the mainstream 'cinedrama'. He considers the importance of 'photogeny', a concept perhaps deriving from the influence of Epstein. He expresses an interest in 'segmentation', perhaps in response to the Russian montage cinema of the period. This critical activity was undertaken alongside Buñuel's work as a film programmer, and fed in turn into the beginnings of his career as a film-maker. From Paris he continued to organize a number of film screenings in Madrid which led to the establishment in 1928 of the Cineclub Español. Fostered by the magazine *La Gaceta Literaria*, it was to become a formative influence upon the development of Spanish film culture in the 1930s. Buñuel's interests as a programmer here and elsewhere ranged from a specialist preoccupation with slow-motion cinematography to a polemical redefinition of cinematic surrealism in terms of classic film comedy.

Buñuel's Entry into Film-making

The critic and programmer soon aspired to become a film-maker in his own right. Letters to friends between July 1927 and August 1928 chronicle a flurry of fretful and unachieved ambitions. A variety of unexplicated half-chances, 'certainties' and mysterious failures issue in just two firm projects. Initially sponsored by the Goya Society of Zaragoza, Buñuel's treatment celebrating the centenary of the painter's death was eventually abandoned for lack of funds. *Los Caprichos*, a multi-story omnibus film, written by Buñuel's favoured collaborator, Ramón Gómez de la Serna, was to have started shooting in Paris in Autumn 1928 on a budget of 25,000 pesetas furnished by Buñuel's mother. *Los Caprichos* was quickly overtaken and eclipsed, however, by the rapid conception and production, in early 1929, of a very different kind of text – Buñuel's first film, *Un Chien Andalou*.

Buñuel's proposed collaboration with Ramón Gómez de la Serna was displaced by cooperation with the young Spanish painter Salvador Dali, whom Buñuel had come to know whilst a student in Madrid. Seemingly consuming the finance intended for *Los Caprichos*, *Un Chien Andalou* was scripted, shot and edited during Spring 1929, enabling it to be premiered at the Studio Ursulines prior to its public run at Studio 28 later in the year. Here it was belatedly discovered and espoused by the official Surrealist group (until Breton managed to catch up with the film, they had been bent upon denunciation of its upstart reputation as a Surrealist work). Buñuel and Dali were rapidly recruited to this vibrant if confused and fickle galaxy.

Writing *Un Chien Andalou*

From correspondence it would appear that Buñuel spent a fortnight at Dali's home in Figueras sometime between January and mid-February 1929, so immersed in the success of their joint productivity – a period 'of total identification' as he remembered it – that he was able to bring forward the start of shooting to March. Dali has recalled rejecting as naïve and sentimental Buñuel's initial idea for a story set in the newspaper world – perhaps *El Mundo por Diez Centimos*, first worked on with Ramón Gómez de la Serna. Instead, they put together a scenario with various working-titles before naming it after Buñuel's first collection of poems, *Un Chien Andalou*. This was a nickname Buñuel and friends had used of those modernist Andalusian poets whom they regarded as insensible to the revolutionary poetry of social content which Buñuel championed. It points to some of the cultural satire Buñuel intended the film to convey. Dali's claim that he presented Buñuel with a complete alternative scenario, scribbled in a quarter of an hour on a shoe-box, does not match Buñuel's memory of the scenario's construction morning-by-morning at Figueras from shared memories of dream-residues and spontaneously invoked gags and objects, a concoction resolutely shorn of 'conscious' meanings and associations.

The only authorial commentary of any prominence occurs in Buñuel's 1929 preface to the first publication of the scenario in *La Révolution Surréaliste*, and, nearly twenty years later, in his 1947 'Notes on the Making of *Un Chien Andalou*'. Here Buñuel offers ambitious and somewhat cloudy contexts for the film. In the 1929 remarks – no more than a brief note – he confirms his adherence to Surrealism, and takes the opportunity to attack those spectators who, recuperating the film as 'beautiful' and 'poetic', overlooked its true intention as a 'desperate and passionate appeal to murder'. The glib terrorism of this finale is mollified in the later *Notes*, but the general project of the film is made little clearer, as, with a kind of threadbare verve, Buñuel contextualizes *Un Chien Andalou* by means of concepts such as 'automaticity', 'the unconscious', 'the poetic', 'the spectator', and the 'avant-garde'.

The 'automaticity' of the film's creation, for Buñuel, cancels 'rational', 'aesthetic' and 'ethical' considerations, together with those of 'customary morality', and points to the fact that *Un Chien Andalou* does not recount a dream but itself 'profits by a mechanism analogous to dreams'. The nature of this mechanism is unclear, but the aesthetic consequence is that the film is able to draw upon putatively 'liberated' psychic impulses, formally deployed as 'poetic' constructs, rather than as 'intended' symbols. In this sense the film is taken as the mark of the film-maker's first production on 'a purely POETICAL-MORAL plane' where 'moral' is taken to be the governing agent in 'dreams or para-sympathetic compulsions'. The shadowy itinerary from the 'unconscious' to the 'poetic' then enables Buñuel to re-write the history of the contemporary cinema. Since the work is marked by deliberately 'anti-plastic' and 'anti-artistic' concerns, it can be seen as 'a violent reaction' against the twenties avant-garde.

Considering the Scenario

Buñuel characterizes the avant-garde as typically directed 'exclusively to the artistic sensibility and to the reason of the spectator, with its play of light and shadow, its photographic effect, its preoccupation with rhythmic montage and technical research, and at times in the direction of the display of a perfectly conventional and reasonable mood'. Buñuel assigns this tendency to the work of Ruttmann, Cavalcanti, Man Ray, Dziga Vertov, René Clair, Germaine Dulac and Joris Ivens. In so doing Buñuel homogenizes the different tendencies of 'documentary' and 'abstract' cinema, traditions clearly calling for far greater differentiation. The reference to Cavalcanti is particularly puzzling, since *Rien que les Heures* had previously elicited Buñuel's praise and sympathy as a reviewer.

Ironically, many of the tendencies Buñuel is attacking here are those avoided in *Un Chien Andalou* not by 'unconscious' creativity at all, but by the choice of a firm pseudo-classical narrative/dramatic baseline for the text. 'Unconscious' film-making would in fact seem to produce the very avant-garde formalism Buñuel is here challenging. This is clearly demonstrated by US avant-gardist Stan Brakhage's later experiments with this method for producing the *Prelude* to his abstract epic *Dog Star Man* (1961), which he based on his mistaken understanding of the 'automatic' production of *Un Chien Andalou*. Strikingly absent, however, from Buñuel's laconic and impressionistic commentaries is any reference to the more obvious and overt structure of the work. *Un Chien Andalou* is to a certain extent a narrative drama. We can read it as a romantic and melodramatic tragicomedy, or a satiric version of the Surrealist *amour fou*. It is a tale of frustrated male desire based on the encounter between a determined 'hero' and a reluctant 'heroine' together with subsidiary dramatic characters. It ends in absurdity and nihilism. This fundamental 'content' is at the same time made more complex, but not displaced, by means of a dazzling repertory of formal tricks and games with cinematic language and convention.

In spite of its commitment to the work of the unconscious, the film in fact has quite deliberate intentions. With familiar Surrealist idealism, Buñuel confers upon the film a strongly conscious sense of purpose when he argues that it makes 'systematic use of the poetic image as an arm to overthrow accepted notions'. And although its makers reject 'intended' symbols, the scenario itself explicitly demands the clear and symbolic placement of objects on the school-desk in the scene with the male protagonist's double (a demand which the film itself does not fulfil with any clarity). We need a more measured commentary than the maker of the film was able to provide, and a less allusive final flourish in the direction of psychoanalysis, to account for the poetics of *Un Chien Andalou*.

From Figueras to Billancourt

In sharp contrast with the creation of the scenario, the process of production in the studio at Billancourt was approached with studied care. Here the spontaneism of 'unconscious' creativity was displaced by the 'conscious' rigours of a two-week shooting schedule, which now involved a team of five or six. Buñuel claims to have gone to work as painstakingly as for an 'historical' film, scene by scene, on a shooting ratio of 3:1. Sadly, Buñuel and Dali tell us nothing of the editing of *Un Chien Andalou*, but it surely took a dramatic and energetic tour de force to pack nearly 300 shots into little over a quarter of an hour with such quick-witted density and powerful onward drive.

Only two actors are formally credited, Simone Mareuil and Pierre Batcheff. Buñuel himself appears as the man with the razor in the opening segment, whilst Dali and the Catalan anarchist Jaime Miratvilles played the part of the priests in segment 7 (although closer examination of these fleeting appearances suggests that, in a typical gesture of discontinuity, three actors may have been involved in the creation of the 'two' screen roles). The only technical credit for *Un Chien Andalou* is awarded to the cinematographer Albert Duverger. The decorator Pierre Schilzneck is associated with set-design for the film – an important contribution in a text hell-bent on playing games with the traditional spatial rules for mise-en-scène, as we shall see. Extras, for the street and park scenes, were rounded up in a local café.

Questions of Iconography

Buñuel wavered between dividing responsibility for this 'automatic' scenario equally between himself and Dali, and assigning his co-scenarist only the famous 'donkeys-and-pianos' segment. This is certainly the aspect of the film Dali remembered best, and on which he appeared to have been most involved during production itself. Dali claims to have kept in close touch with the production through nightly conversations with a deferential Buñuel, but seems to have been active in the studio itself only for the donkeys-and-pianos segment. Dali's contribution appears to have been symptomatically feverish and grisly. As he reminisced in *The Secret Life*, Dali worked on the set like a painter or a sculptor, emptying and enlarging the donkeys' eye-sockets, cutting away at their mouths to emphasize the teeth, and adding supplementary jaw-bones 'so that it would appear that, although the donkeys were already rotting, they were still vomiting up a little more of their own death, above those other rows of teeth formed by the keys of the black piano'.

The dead and putrefying donkey was a sight Buñuel and Dali would have encountered in Spanish rural life; it is an early, powerful reference-point in Buñuel's autobiography. The donkey is visible – peripherally and sometimes even spectrally – in Dali's paintings as early as 'Senecitas' (1926), 'Apparatus and Hand' (1927) and 'Blood is Sweeter than Honey' (1927). It is an icon which can equally be discovered in Dali's verbal art, where the 'putrid' donkey features in a number of the 1927–8 poems. Perhaps Dali's most striking manipulation of the image, interesting not only for its connection with *Un Chien Andalou* and *L'Age d'Or* but for its evidence of the Surrealists' confused interests in psychoanalysis, occurs in the 1930 prose text 'L'Ane Pourri', which asserts a relationship between paranoia and the perception of double and multiple images. Pianos, on the other hand, become frequent icons in Dali's paintings rather later than *Un Chien Andalou*, largely in the period 1931–6, with such paintings as 'Six Apparitions of Lenin on a Pianoforte', 'Invisible Harp', 'Skull with Its Lyric Appendage Leaning on a Night Table which Should Have the Temperature of a Cardinal's Nest', and 'Three Young Surrealist Women Holding in their Arms the Skins of an Orchestra'. 'Sodomy Committed by a Skull with a Grand Piano' is particularly reminiscent of *Un Chien Andalou*.

Just as Dali appears to portray himself, in explicit or attenuated form, in many of his 1929–30 paintings, so he inscribes himself ironically into the character of one of the pair of priests in the donkeys-and-pianos segment. (Buñuel, for his part, occasionally impersonated priests in real life.) Dali regularly includes 'repetitive forms' within his paintings – nowhere, however, as conspicuously as in the large-scale examples of 'twinning' to be found in the donkeys-and-pianos segment, which range from the 'double burden' hauled by the male protagonist to the local duplication of teeth and jaw-bones noted earlier. Dali was abidingly preoccupied with anatomical surrealism. His fascination with bone-structures (chiefly skulls), climaxing in the period 1933–4, can be plausibly attributed to his familiarity with Picasso's work.

As far as the gigantic 'machine' featured in this segment is concerned – grand pianos, dead donkeys, melons, floats, ropes, and priests – it is worth noting that the outcome of Dali's encounter with Picasso's lack of reverence for traditional media, in particular the example of his collages, was Dali's execution, on his return to Spain from a trip to Paris in 1928, of several huge abstract canvases from which stones and all manner of heavy objects were suspended by thick cords. Dali's own fertile memories do not clarify exactly what Picasso showed him of his work during their encounter, but it seems likely that the work he went on to produce represents the same series of twenty collage-reliefs on white backgrounds, most of which were subsequently thrown away because his parents saw nothing in them except a few stones, a few pieces of rope, and some tiny ideographic signs.

It would be wrong, however, to envisage iconographic meanings for the segment solely in relation to the work of Dali. The seeds of this complex and absurd creation perhaps also lie in other sources. In Buñuel's autobiography, for example, he remembers from his child-hood a cartoon from the violently anti-clerical and pro-anarchist journal *El Mitón*, involving 'two well-fed priests sitting in a small cart while Christ, harnessed to the shafts, sweats and grimaces with the effort'. Looking to the film more broadly, it may of course prove illuminating to trace the links between the ants that swarm in Dali's paintings and the ants of *Un Chien Andalou*. It may obviously be valuable to make connections between the opening of *Un Chien Andalou* and the fund of lacerated eyes to be found in Surrealist imagery more generally, as well as with the woman's eye savaged by a Cossack sabre in *The Battleship Potemkin*, long one of Buñuel's favourite films. But it would take a powerful theory of iconography, and of film meaning, to explain in any detail their functioning within a text as insistent upon the routine deconstruction of the image as *Un Chien Andalou*.

Exhibition and Circulation

In terms of distribution and exhibition the privately-financed *Un Chien Andalou* can embark without peril upon the normally perilous trajectory of the 'short' film (although the 'two-reeler', as Buñuel consciously saw *Un Chien Andalou*, enjoyed a more privileged status within film exhibition patterns than today, as is suggested by the film's early opportunity for an extended public run of some eight months, which earned Buñuel 7–8,000 francs). For its main authors, the film marks a cultural and social immigration (from Spain to France) and a clear cultural entrée (into Parisian Surrealism). Specifically, it is Buñuel's route to feature-film production (*L'Age d'Or* in 1930) and a stepping-stone in Dali's rapid rise to celebrity and notoriety as a Surrealist painter (his first Paris exhibition, at the Goémans Gallery, coinciding with a late stage in the public run of *Un Chien Andalou*).

Fittingly, in the case of a film preoccupied with processes of transformation, the production history of *Un Chien Andalou* does not stop short in 1929. In 1960, the film entered a new stage in its textual and social history. At this point it was bought by Raymond Rohauer, key exploiter of the silent cinema, and a music-track was added – under Buñuel's supervision – recreating the 1929 gramophone accompaniment. In terms of British film culture, however, it still remained caught between the 'credit' of its aesthetic pedigree, and the notoriety engendered by its lack of a certificate for public exhibition. In 1968, after nearly forty years of clandestine existence, it was finally deemed suitable for adult audiences and received an 'X' certificate.

In this period, the infamy of *Un Chien Andalou*'s 'excessive' surrealism was perhaps mollified by Buñuel's increasing acceptance into mainstream European arthouse film culture, a process helped by the auteurist vogue which coincided with the triumph of *Viridiana* in 1960. In this period, *Un Chien Andalou* also bore the larger burden of representing the early Buñuel thanks to the long-standing unavailability, because of copyright problems, of his key debut feature, *L'Age d'Or*. In 1982, the film was reinterpreted by a later modernism, when Swiss TV commissioned the composer Mauricio Kagel to create a new soundtrack, featuring strings and sound-tape. Kagel makes literal the film's title by introducing dog calls here and there, with varying dramatic implications.

Un Chien Andalou: Surrealist Text

Un Chien Andalou is an intense amalgam of modernist material drawn from a wide variety of cultural sources. Its textual orientations are ambiguous and fluid. It has 'characters' of sorts who are involved together in some kind of 'story', but in the fictional world of Buñuel and Dali they are of little more importance than the surreally grotesque and absurd cinematic signs upon which the film equally depends for its spectacle and its effects. On the one hand it relates to, and yet also turns away from, the traditional textual apparatus of the mainstream narrative film. We might refer to this in shorthand as the 'classic realism' of the mainstream text, in which clearly identifiable characters act out a human drama in the logical pursuit of clear-cut psychological or practical goals. Yet, although *Un Chien Andalou* has no real interest in this traditional model, it does not opt for any clear alternative. It does not lapse, for instance, into the resolutely poetic 'impressionism' or 'abstractionism' of the contemporary French avant-garde, against which Buñuel and Dali were equally and consciously reacting. Rather, the film prefers to mix both streams of influence, and is thus of special interest precisely as an ambiguous turning point between the alternatives of dominant and counter-cinema.

Comedy and Melodrama

Un Chien Andalou shares a broad intertextuality with a range of cinematic genres popular in the twenties – the romance, the melodrama and the comedy. The chief figure in this intertextual relation is the film's male lead, Pierre Batcheff, with his involvement in the traditions of cinematic stardom. We can detect in *Un Chien Andalou* a parody of the previous romantic roles of Batcheff, in particular, perhaps, *The Siren of the Tropics*, in which Buñuel and Duverger had been involved. In the scenario, furthermore, the protagonist is explicitly required to assume the mien of 'a traitor out of melodrama', a lead taken up by critics who responded to the film's critique of the pantomime qualities of silent-movie drama and, at the same time, to its fulfilment of some of the narrative requirements of a popular thriller.

This hypothesis is strengthened by the physical resemblance between Batcheff and another silent hero, Buster Keaton. The likelihood of Keaton's influence on an elaborate gag and pratfall in the donkeys-and-pianos segment has not gone unnoticed. It is worth recalling that Buñuel had ardently reviewed Keaton's *College* in 1927, to the extent of drawing up an international typology for acting styles on the basis of his enthusiasm for Keaton. Perhaps it would not be too far-fetched to see this segment as in some sense an attempt to re-stage Keaton's own efforts to haul a piano into his new and equally unstable marital home in *One Week* (1920).

European and American Comedy

Buñuel's typology was made up of a binary opposition between European and American acting styles. He differentiated between the essentially expressionistic style of what he christened the 'School of Jannings' – a European lineage, also including John Barrymore, Conrad Veidt and Mosjukhin, characterized by 'sentimentality, prejudices of art, literature, tradition' – and the triumphantly American 'School of Buster Keaton' – exemplified by Monte Blue, Laura la Plante, Bebe Daniels, Tom Moore, Adolph Menjou and Harry Langdon – whose style suggested 'vitality, photogeny, no culture and new tradition'. An homage to Keaton would therefore by no means have been out of place for Buñuel and Dali, whose friend the poet and dramatist Lorca had written his own tribute the previous year, 'El Paseo de Buster Keaton' – a work which shares some general affinities with *Un Chien Andalou*.

Buñuel's personal enthusiasm for the 'surrealist commitment' in the commericial cinema, the 'genuine surrealism' of film comedy, may be gauged from his programme of comic cinema for the Cine-club Español in May 1930. The programme, an anthology of the work of more than a dozen comedians, was billed as the first of its kind in a European cineclub. *Un Chien Andalou* itself appears to have run at the Studio 28 in Autumn 1929 on the same bill as an early Harold Lloyd comedy (permitting one contemporary critic to prefer what he saw as the 'condensed witticism' of an authentic American comedy to European Surrealist derivatives).

Character Relations

The film depends upon a central male-female relationship, played out by its two named stars, but their characters do not have names, are hardly ever seen to speak and are psychologically and physio-logically inconsistent. The Batcheff character, for instance, appears in three 'states' in the film: as 'himself', as his 'double' and as a cyclist in maid's costume. There are three important subsidiary characters: the man with the razor in the 'prologue'; the new woman in the street; and the new male lover whom the female protagonist encounters at the seaside. Only the last-named enters into 'realist' relations with a central character. The second offers a kind of 'side-show' which impacts on the central couple by inspiring the male protagonist to still greater personal ardour; the first appears, in his assault upon the eye of the female protagonist, to threaten her survival beyond the 'prologue' (but this does not happen, and in this curious fiction she happily outlives her assailant).

While the relationship between the two main characters centres on the female protagonist's resistance to the male protagonist's ministr-ations and attempted seduction, the sexual progress of the narrative is initiated obliquely. It opens with a 'prologue' which features the female protagonist suffering an horrendous mutilation – which, incomprehensibly, does not mark her in the remainder of the film. Her relation to the male protagonist is negotiated indirectly, by a series of obscure gifts and visions (the delivery of a mysterious box; the female protagonist's mourning over the cyclist's disembodied costume; the couple's 'vision' of a subsidiary female character; the male protagonist's grotesque burden of donkeys, pianos and other paraphernalia hauled towards the central female character). It is a relation which subsides into fantastic physical competition – the male central character erasing his own mouth and replacing it with hair magically transferred from the armpit of the female protagonist – before culminating in the shock of a magical transition from the city to the seaside. It concludes with the couple's sudden and unexpected burial in an unknown landscape.

Character, Figure, Body

It is indeed the male protagonist, in his various states, who most clearly exceeds the normal bounds of characterization. As himself, he can produce a swarm of ants out of a hole in the centre of his palm; can produce from nowhere a grotesque conglomeration of corks, melons, priests and pianos bearing dead and rotting donkeys, bound together with huge ropes; can transform school-books, thanks to a metaphoric jump-cut, into murderous revolvers; can erase his mouth and replace it with the body hair of a woman he is seeking to impress. As his double, he can traverse an impossible distance, bedroom to park, all in a dying fall. In a film where identities appear to merge and are sometimes difficult to distinguish, it is in any case a conclusion whose narrative surprise is further inflected by the more than momentary and crucial difficulty posed, by the nature of the concluding shot, in recognizing the male figure as the 'main' protagonist rather than the 'new' lover of the previous segment. The female protagonist, throughout, poses no such difficulties for recognition.

These quasi-magical abilities are linked to the film's obsessive blurring and destruction of the human form. The eye of the female protagonist is sliced open with a razor in the 'prologue' and yet is intact throughout the remainder of the film; the torso of the female protagonist dissolves into naked breasts and then into naked buttocks under the male protagonist's only 'successful' caress; a pair of priests are turned into human lumber; the naked woman in the park dissolves away into invisibility upon a touch from the male protagonist's 'double'; the main couple are cut in half by burial up to the waist in the final shot; a chain of severed or seemingly autonomous hands eerily punctuate the film. In the final shot (although it is difficult to perceive in the finished film) the scenario tells us that the buried couple have been blinded – returning us to a grim bodily motif introduced at the very outset. The film's discontinuous vision of the human body is thus connected to its overall explosion of psychological–dramatic logic and coherence in the cinema.

Subsidiary Characters

Mirroring the instability of the central character–relationship, subsidiary characters are interpolated without obvious internal logic and without fictional contextualization. They play their roles, then disappear. The film thus opens with a notorious 'prologue', in which the female protagonist encounters a man who, in addition to inflicting mysterious and horrific injury upon her (with her seeming collusion), will not reappear in the remainder of the film. The central couple will be interrupted by the view from their window of a second female character in the street below, so preoccupied with a severed hand that she is run over by a car as she day-dreams, closing off her story. The male protagonist will be visited by his 'double', whom he shoots dead. As he falls dying – transported into parkland by means of the 'creative geography' of film editing – he clutches at the averted body of a naked woman, who herself disappears when he touches her. As late as the penultimate segment of the film, the female protagonist will, with no narrative warning given, encounter a new lover. Mocking the aberrant time-structure of the film, he will indicate his displeasure at what is for him her late arrival, only to be immediately jettisoned himself for the film to end on a different surprise again.

Specifying Time: The Inter-Titles

The flexibility of this structure, in which psychological naturalism and conventional dramatic logic have been displaced, predictably affects the temporal and spatial organization of the text. If we trust to the presumed authority of inter-titles, for example, the film would appear to be segmented into five main, temporally definite passages; but the inter-titles fluctuate between extreme specificity and extreme generality: 'Once upon a time . . .'; 'Eight Years Later'; 'Towards Three in the Morning . . .'; 'Sixteen Years Before'; 'In the Spring . . .'; In the process, they also divide the film into extremely varying lengths and temporal durations. The final title is not a truly separate inter-title but dissolves in and out of the film during the final image, holding its own screen-space for a while. Its apparent verbal promise – 'In the Spring . . .' – of course contradicts the morbidity of the imagery of death the shot contains.

The fourth title, 'Sixteen Years Before', seems to punctuate a larger continuous segment – intervening in the male protagonist's confrontation with his double – rather than initiating a new segment of its own, pointing to the irregularity of this form of segmentation in the film as a whole. Thus the 'prologue' is extremely difficult to read as an introduction to the film, while the later segment which follows on from the death of the male protagonist's 'double', focusing attention for some time on his cortège, appears to be about to close the film, only for the film to promptly start again. The prepossessing intrusion of the 'double' is thus contextualized in retrospect as no more than a momentary displacement of the central character-axis. When the film finally succeeds in ending, it does so via an image totally deprived, like the 'prologue', of logical connection and explanation within the body of the film.

Surreal Space

The textual space of *Un Chien Andalou* is as perturbed as its temporal organization. Locations, for example, accumulate discretely, by a process of simple addition rather than by typically realist systems of re-permutation and re-cycling. Emblematic in this respect is the final location, the desert sprouting half-buried acquaintances, introduced for the first time in what is effectively the film's closing shot. More striking still is the example of the bedroom and the balcony which provide the location for the 'prologue'. This only serves to underline the enigmatic nature of this segment when, like its first 'character' (the man with the razor), this location never reappears, except via parallels – the bedroom which stages the main action, the window through which the street-scene will be watched and the cyclist's clothing hurled.

In the 'prologue', for example, there is no clear and explicit location for the female protagonist, when she appears in facial close-ups only. These shots may express the 'imaginary' vision of the temporary protagonist, the man with the razor, rather than denoting her 'real' presence at this stage of the narrative. Less dramatically, the pair of hands which activate a cocktail-shaker instead of the expected door-bell when the male protagonist's 'double' pays a visit are a surreal substitution which the film refuses to locate in any spatial context. They float between mere narrative association with the caller in the doorway and with the face of the 'host', itself increasingly dis-located in the previous segment.

More curious is the fusion of a pair of shots which brings together, thanks to a dissolve, what the scenario describes (but which is difficult to visually identify) as a sunbather's armpit (shot 62) with a sea-urchin accompanied by a single human footprint (shot 63). These are images which the film has not prepared us for, and which introduce a geographic location which is difficult to construe (the seashore?). They can be recontextualized by the later beach-scene, although these 'anticipations' themselves do not reappear. Widely separated spaces are regularly bridged by a defiant continuity of actions. When the 'double' dies, he collapses in the bedroom but hits the ground in an as yet unseen woodland location. In another earth-shrinking cut, the female protagonist flounces out of the bedroom straight onto the seashore, itself improbably including a background of only one of the shots which make up this segment.

Sometimes this playfulness blurs traditional distinctions between interior and exterior space through an emphasis upon the visionary power of eyesight – a trope central to the 'prologue' and to the couple's interest in the scene down in the street below their building. A subtler version of this tendency is represented by the film's continual play with vision in relation to the maintenance or disturbance of filmic space through eyeline-matches and mis-matches and looks directed on-screen and off-screen. The look of the female protagonist brings up an image of the cyclist to a point directly opposite her room, and on a level with it, even though the cyclist has not yet reached the building, and the apartment is located on at least the first floor above street-level, as subsequent high-angle shots quite clearly insist.

This is the location where point-of-view shots may be played with to the point of complete inversion. The interior of the room will somehow – even to the surprise of the characters themselves – find space to produce, as though out of thin air, the monstrous burden hauled by the protagonist towards his love-object. It is a room which, once escaped, can itself – like other elements within the film – spawn a double, as the female protagonist finds out to her dismay when she escapes the donkeys and pianos. Later, the room erases her on her way to open a door, so that it opens as though automatically for a visitor.

In this surprising space – considerably in advance of the wily sleight of hand of Ozu or of the magically mobile throne of King

Sigismund in the opening moments of Eisenstein's *The Boyars Plot* –
the furniture and fittings seemingly move around at will, unbal-
ancing spatial relationships within what has previously appeared to
be a fixed and confined arena. This process is extended by the film's
interest in such techniques as superimposition (shot 22), flash-
framing within continuous action (shot 47), jump-cuts and internal
dissolves creating magical metamorphoses within the image (shots
49, 51, 226), slow-motion and grain (shots 213–217). Irises and
dissolves are used to make pictorial-conceptual bridges between
shots and segments (the series 61–4) or to enact seemingly 'subjective' vision whilst retaining 'objective' viewpoint (shots 114–124). In
general, camera-angles and the composition of the image often
emphasize the graphic and material presence of the film frame itself
(for example, in shots 27, 36, 81, 87, 102).

The Work of Sound

The nature of the sound-track for *Un Chien Andalou*, recreated in
1960 in an archival gesture commemorating Buñuel's original
gramophone accompaniment, further complicates analysis of the
film. The musical accompaniment is based on a binary opposition
between Wagnerian romanticism (the *Liebestod* from *Tristan and
Isolde*) and popular South American dance music (a pair of Argentinian tangos). Internally patterned via alternation and repetition,
the music, on the whole, both endorses the segmentation which
obeys the inter-titles, but at the same time also re-groups larger
segments in the film. These five 'new' segments (see transcription for
particulars) are thus equal in number to the segments formed by the
chain of inter-titles, but different again in shape and size.

Displacing dialogue – even when characters are, very occasionally,
seen to 'speak' – the music, at its own level of abstraction, both
supports and undermines the images. The music for the death of
Isolde will thus 'match' the depicted deaths of two of the characters –
the new woman in the street and the male protagonist's double – but,
ironically, the major rather than the subsidiary characters will enjoy
no such musical reinforcement. The male protagonist's pursuit of
the female protagonist can thus be satirized by a tango. In a further
gesture of distanciation and separation, it is the light-hearted vigour
of the tango which will cover the gloomy business of the 'prologue',
and the female protagonist's interment, with the male protagonist, at

he end. The film thus opens and closes on inscrutably violent events which are further mystified by the apparent nonchalance of their musical accompaniment. By doubling up on closure – the *Liebestod* nding on the fading of the 'double's' cortège – the music-track can, qually deceptively, appear to close a film which immediately recommences'. Its Wagnerian sentiment is again displaced by the ango which sees the film through the three remaining segments to ts 'true' finale.

Rereading *Un Chien Andalou*

The surrealism of *Un Chien Andalou* cannot be reduced to the ssumed intentions of its makers Buñuel and Dali, given the role of he unconscious, and of chance, in the way they compiled its cenario. In turn, however, it cannot be simplified to myths of utomatic production, since the inspirational manner in which its cenario was produced was not replicated in the act of film production, where a more measured and deliberate activity was undertaken n the studio. Furthermore, it should not be entirely collapsed into he concerns of Surrealism at large, since the film preceded its maker's acceptance into the movement, and imposed its own variant f Surrealism upon the official discourse of the group. And finally, it annot be subordinated to the harmonizing quest of another critical radition, bent on simplifying the film's production of meaning in erms of a primitive thematic and psychoanalytic reading.

This dominant critical tradition has sought global meanings, table and immutable, which explain the film as an allegory of exuality, or of childhood, or of modern alienation. This is based on he erroneous view of Surrealism as merely a complex form of aturalism, of symbolization in the cinema, as simply the practice of lenotation shifted to the distance of a single remove. The surrealism f *Un Chien Andalou* will make poor sense if abandoned to such nterpretative determination. Rather, the film's contribution to the oetics of Surrealism lies in its relentless semiotic work on these asic cultural themes. Its surrealism, in other words, is the material roduction of the film's specific play of difference, contradiction nd re-contextualization as we have described it here. It is within his reflexive textuality that the film's modernism must henceforth e understood.

PHILIP DRUMMOND, 1994

Foreword

Un Chien Andalou, though primarily a subjective drama fashioned into a poem, is none the less, in my opinion, a film of social consciousness.

Un Chien Andalou is a masterwork from every aspect: its certainty of direction, its brilliance of lighting, its perfect amalgam of visual and ideological associations, its sustained dreamlike logic, its admirable confrontation between the subconscious and the rational.

Considered in terms of social consciousness, *Un Chien Andalou* is both precise and courageous.

Incidentally I would like to make the point that it belongs to an extremely rare class of film.

I have met M. Luis Buñuel only once and then only for ten minutes, and our meeting in no way touched upon *Un Chien Andalou*. This enables me to discuss it with that much greater liberty. Obviously my comments are entirely personal. Possibly I will get near the truth, without doubt I will commit some howlers.

In order to understand the significance of the film's title it is essential to remember that M. Buñuel is Spanish.

An Andalusian dog howls – who then is dead?

Our cowardice, which leads us to accept so many of the horrors that we, as a species, commit, is dearly put to the test when we flinch from the screen image of a woman's eye sliced in half by a razor. Is it more dreadful than the spectacle of a cloud veiling a full moon?

Such is the prologue: it leaves us with no alternative but to admit that we will be committed, that in this film we will have to view with something more than the everyday eye.

Throughout the film we are held in the same grip.

From the first sequence we discern, beneath the image of an over-grown child riding up the street without touching the handlebars, hands on his thighs, covered with white frills like so many wings, we discern, I repeat, our truth which turns to cowardice in contact with the world which we accept, (one gets the world one deserves), this world of inflated prejudices, of betrayals of one's inner self, of pathetically romanticized regrets.

M. Buñuel is a fine marksman who disdains the stab in the back.

A kick in the pants to macabre ceremonies, to those last rites for a being no longer there, who has become no more than a dust-filled hollow down the centre of the bed.

A kick in the pants to those who have sullied love by resorting to rape.

A kick in the pants to sadism, of which buffoonery is its most disguised form.

And let us pluck a little at the reins of morality with which we harness ourselves.

Let's see a bit of what is at the end.

A cork, here is a weighty argument.

A melon – the disinherited middle classes.

Two priests – alas for Christ!

Two grand pianos, stuffed with corpses and excrement – our pathetic sentimentality.

Finally, the donkey in close-up. We were expecting it.

M. Buñuel is terrible.

Shame on those who kill in youth what they themselves would have become, who seek, in the forests and along the beaches, where the sea casts up our memories and regrets the dried-up projection of their first blossoming.
Cave canem . . .

All this written in an attempt to avoid too arid an analysis, image by image, in any case impossible in a good film whose savage poetry exacts respect – and with the sole aim of creating the desire to see or see again *Un Chien Andalou*. To cultivate a socially aware cinema is to ensure a cinema which deals with subjects which provoke interest, of subjects which cut ice . . .

JEAN VIGO in 'Vers un cinéma social,' 1930

Un Chien Andalou

Credits

THE YOUNG WOMAN   Simone Mareuil
THE MAN   Pierre Batcheff
OTHERS   Jaime Miratvilles, Salvador Dali,
   Luis Buñuel

Produced by   Luis Buñuel
Script by   Luis Buñuel and Salvador Dali
Directed by   Luis Buñuel
Photographed by   Albert Duverger
Décor   Pierre Schilzneck

Left to right: Dali, Buñuel, Simone Mareuil, Jeanne Rucas (Buñuel's future wife) and Pierre Batcheff.

Original Shooting Script
by Luis Buñuel and Salvador Dali

ONCE UPON TIME . . .
A balcony. Night. A man is sharpening a razor by the balcony.
The man looks through a window at the sky and sees . . .
A light cloud passing across the face of the full moon.
Then the head of a young woman with wide-open eyes. The blade of
the razor moves towards one of her eyes.
The light cloud now moves across the face of the moon. The razor-
blade slices the eye of the young woman, dividing it.

EIGHT YEARS LATER
A deserted road. It is raining.
A man, dressed in a dark-grey suit and riding a bicycle, appears. The
man's head, back and waist are decked in white frills. A rectangular
box with black-and-white diagonal stripes hangs from a thong on his
chest. The man's feet pedal automatically and he is not holding the
handlebars: his hands are resting on his knees. Medium shot of him
seen from behind, then shot of him superimposed on shot of the
street, down which he is cycling with his back to camera. He cycles
towards camera until the striped box fills the screen.
A room on the third floor of a building overlooking the street. A
young woman in a brightly-coloured dress is sitting in the centre of
the room; she is absorbed in reading a book. She gives a start, listens
for something and throws the book onto a nearby couch. The book
remains opened on a reproduction of Vermeer's 'The Lace-Maker'.
The young woman is now convinced that something interesting is
taking place; she gets up, half-turns and walks quickly over to the
window. The cyclist has just stopped, below in the street. Out of
sheer inertia, without trying to keep his balance, he topples over into
the muddy gutter.
The young woman, looking resentful and outraged, dashes out of the
room and down the stairs.
Close-up of the cyclist lying on the ground, expressionless, in exactly
the same position as when he fell.

3

The young woman runs out of the house towards him and throws herself on him to kiss him passionately on the lips, the eyes and the nose.

It is now raining so hard that the rain blots out what is happening on screen.

Dissolve to the box: its diagonal stripes are superimposed on the diagonal lines of falling rain. Hands holding a little key open the box and pull out a tie wrapped in striped tissue paper.

The rain, the box, the tissue paper, and the tie make up a pattern of diagonal stripes of varying sizes.

The same room.

The young woman is standing by the bed, looking at the various items worn by the cyclist – frilly cuffs, box, starched collar and plain black tie. All these things are laid out on the bed as though they were being worn by someone lying on the bed. The young woman finally decides to reach out and she picks up the collar, removes the plain tie from it, and puts in its place the striped tie which she has just taken out of the box. She then puts the collar back where it was and sits down by the bed like someone at a vigil. The blanket and pillow on the bed are slightly rumpled as though a body really was lying there.

The young woman seems to be aware of someone standing behind her and she turns to see who it is. Without showing any surprise, she sees that it is the same man, no longer wearing any of the items that are laid out on the bed. He is looking at something on his right palm with great concentration and some distress.

The young woman goes over to him and also looks at what he has in his hand.

Close-up of the hand full of ants crawling out of a black hole in the palm. None of the ants fall off.

Dissolve to the hairs on the armpit of a young woman who is lying on a beach in the sunshine. Dissolve to the undulating spines of a sea-urchin. Dissolve to the head of a girl seen directly from above. This shot is taken as though through the iris of an eye: the iris opens to reveal a group of people standing around the girl and trying to push their way through a police barrier.

In the middle of the circle, the young girl is using a stick to try and pick up a severed hand with painted fingernails which is lying on the ground. A policeman goes up to her and begins rebuking her. He leans down, picks up the hand, wraps it up carefully and puts it inside the striped box which had been hanging round the cyclist's

4

neck. He hands the box over to the girl; she thanks him and he salutes.

As the policeman gives her the box, she seems to be completely carried away by a strange emotion and is oblivious of everything that is going on around her. It is as though she were listening to some distant religious music, perhaps music she heard when she was a child.

The crowd's curiosity has died down. People are moving off in all directions.

The couple has been looking at the scene from behind the window on the third floor all this time. We can see them through the window, from which we too have been watching the end of the scene. When the policeman gives the box to the young girl, the two people in the room also seem overwhelmed with the same emotion. They nod as though in rhythm to that distant music which only the young girl can hear.

The man looks at the young woman and makes a gesture as though to say, 'You see? Didn't I tell you?'

She looks down at the street again, where the young girl, all alone now, stands as if rooted to the spot, incapable of moving, as cars drive past her at great speed. Suddenly one of the cars runs her over and leaves her lying in the street, horribly mangled.

The man, with the determination of someone who feels sure of his rights, goes over to the young woman and, after staring at her lustfully with rolling eyes, grabs her breasts through her dress. Close-up of the man's hands fondling the breasts which appear through the dress. The man's face has a terrible look, almost of mortal anguish, and a stream of blood-flecked saliva begins to run out of the corner of his mouth onto the naked breasts. The breasts disappear to become a pair of thighs which the man kneads.

His expression has changed. His eyes now shine with cruelty and lust. His mouth, which was wide open, now puckers up like an anus. The young woman moves back towards the centre of the room, followed by the man, still in the same state.

She suddenly breaks his hold on her and escapes from his grasp. The man's mouth tightens with anger. The young woman realizes that a really disagreeable and violent scene is about to take place. She inches away until she reaches a corner of the room where she crouches behind a little table.

The man, now looking like the villain in a melodrama, looks around,

5

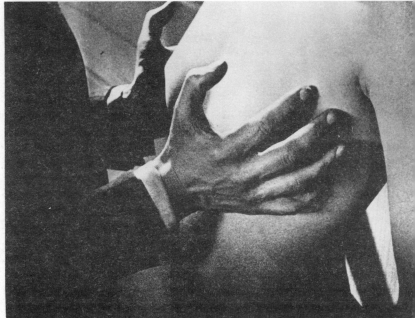

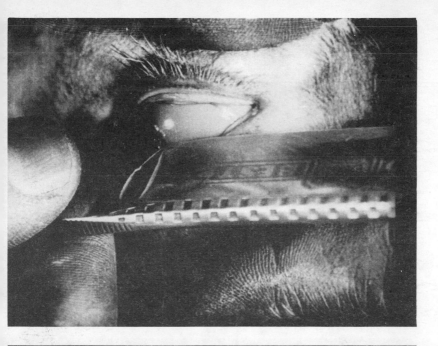

trying to find something. He sees a piece of rope lying on the floor and picks it up with his right hand. He then gropes about with his left hand and picks up another identical piece of rope.

The young woman, glued to the wall, looks with horror at what he is doing.

The man begins advancing towards her, pulling at the rope and making a great effort to drag whatever is attached to the ropes.

First we see a cork, then a melon, then two Catholic priests, then finally, two magnificent grand pianos containing the carcasses of two donkeys. Their feet, tails, rumps and excrement are spilling out of the lids. As one of the grand pianos is pulled past the camera, we can see the big head of one of the donkeys hanging down over the keyboard. The man pulls at this with great difficulty, straining desperately towards the young woman, knocking over chairs, tables, a standing lamp and other objects in his path. The rumps of the donkeys get caught in everything. A stripped bone hits the light hanging from the ceiling, so that it rocks from side to side until the end of the scene.

When the man is just about to reach the young woman, she rushes out of the room. Her attacker lets go of the ropes and hurls himself after her. The young woman manages to get out of the room into the next one, but not quickly enough to slam the door shut. The man's hand is trapped in the door, caught in the jamb.

In the other room, the young woman pulls harder and harder at the door, watching the fingers of the hand moving painfully and slowly as the ants begin crawling out of the palm onto the door. The young woman turns away to look at the room, which is identical to the previous one except that different lighting gives it a different appearance: the young woman . . .

The same bed is there, with the same man lying on it, the one who has still got his hand in the door. He is wearing the frills and the box lies on his chest. He does not move at all, but stares with wide-open eyes which seem to be saying, 'Something really extraordinary is just about to happen!'

AT THREE O'CLOCK IN THE MORNING
A stranger, seen from the back, is stopping on the landing outside the apartment. He rings the bell. Unlike in other silent films of the period, we do not see the actual electric bell ringing inside the room. Instead, we see two hands shaking a silver cocktail shaker through

two holes cut in the door, immediately after the doorbell has been rung.

The man lying on the bed in the room gives a start. The young woman goes to open the door.

The stranger goes directly over to the bed and commands the man lying down to get up. The man is so reluctant to do this that the stranger is obliged to grab his cuffs and force him to rise.

The newcomer tears off the man's frills one by one and hurls them out of the window along with the striped box and the thong which the man tries vainly to save from the catastrophe. He then orders the man to go and stand against one of the walls of the room as a punishment.

The stranger has done all this with his back to the camera. Only now does he turn around for the first time to go and fetch something in another part of the room.

At that instant, the shot goes out of focus. The stranger moves in slow motion and we see that his features are identical to those of the first man. They are the same person, except that the stranger is younger, more full of pathos, rather like the man must have been many years earlier.

SIXTEEN YEARS BEFORE

The stranger walks across the room, while the camera tracks back to reveal him in medium close-up. He is walking towards an old school desk which now comes into shot. There are various school things lying about on the desk, including two books. The placing of the objects must have a clear and symbolic meaning.

The stranger picks up the books and turns to go back towards the man. In that instant, the shot ceases to be out of focus and in slow motion, and goes back to normal.

When the stranger reaches the spot where the other man is standing, he orders him to stretch out his arms in the shape of a cross and places a book in each of the man's hands, ordering him to keep this position as a punishment.

The man looks vicious and treacherous as he turns to face the stranger. The books he is holding begin to change into two revolvers.

The stranger looks at the man with an expression of ever-increasing tenderness.

The man threatens the stranger with his guns, forcing him to put his

9

hands up. In spite of this, the first man fires both revolvers.

Medium close-up of the stranger falling to the ground, mortally wounded, an expression of pain contorting his features (the photography is once again out of focus and in even slower motion).

In the distance, we see the wounded man, no longer inside the room, but in a park. By him sits a woman with bare shoulders, her back turned to the camera, leaning slightly forward.

As he falls, the wounded man tries to grasp and stroke the woman's bare shoulders; one of his trembling hands is turned inwards, while the other lightly claws at the bare skin. The man finally falls to the ground.

Long shot: a few passers-by and a policeman rush over to the man, pick him up and carry him off through the woods, just as a lame man comes into shot.

Cut back to the same room. The door in which the man's hand was caught now opens slowly. The young woman appears. She closes the door behind her and carefully examines the wall against which the murderer was just standing.

The man is no longer there. The wall is blank; there is no furniture nor decoration on it. The young woman makes a gesture of annoyance and impatience.

Shot of the wall again. There is a small black spot in the middle of it. This little spot, seen closer in, is a death's head moth. Close-up of the moth, large close-up of the death's head on its back. The death's head covers the whole screen.

Medium close-up of the man who was wearing the frills. He suddenly claps his hand to his mouth as though his teeth were falling out. The young woman looks at him disdainfully. When the man takes his hand away, we see his mouth has disappeared. The young woman seems to say to him, 'Well, and afterwards?' Then she redoes her lips with her lipstick. On the man's face, hairs are growing in the place where his mouth used to be. When the young woman notices, she stifles a cry and quickly looks at her armpit which is completely hairless. She scornfully thrusts out her tongue at the man, throws a shawl over her shoulders and opens the door. She walks out of the door into the next room which is a vast beach.

A man is waiting by the edge of the sea. This man and the young woman seem happy to see each other; they wander off together down the beach, following the waterline.

Shot of their legs and the waves at their feet.

Camera tracks after the couple. The waves gently wash up the thong, the striped box, the frills and, last of all, the bicycle. Camera remains fixed for a while, even though nothing more is being washed ashore. The two people wander down the beach, gradually fading from view as the following words appear in the sky:

IN THE SPRING
Everything has changed. We now see a limitless desert; the man and the young woman are in the centre of the screen, buried up to their chests in sand, blinded, in rags, being eaten alive by the sun and by swarms of insects.

Transcription of the Film

All shots are separated by cuts unless otherwise stated.

The music-track is made up on alternation between Wagner and a pair of Argentinian tangos. Commencing with the tango four seconds into the film, the sequence is: tango (credit titles, segment 1), Wagner (segments 2 to mid-7), tango (mid-7 to 9), Wagner (10 to 11), tango (12 to 14). In the course of the film, we hear the Liebestod *from* Tristan and Isolde *in its entirety: Shot 14 to mid-108, beginning to third beat of bar 65; Shots 211 to 254, fourth beat of bar to end.*

Running-time: 16 minutes 18 seconds.

Credit Sequence

i   Rolling credit in French, white lettering on black background featuring the logo of the Guilde Internationale du Disque. [English translation:

> 'The music for this film is drawn from recordings
> by the
> Guilde Internationale du Disque
> *Tristan and Isolde* by Richard Wagner is performed
> by the Orchestra of the Frankfurt Opera
> under the direction of Carl Bamberger
> The creation of the sound-track for the integral
> version of this film was carried out in 1960
> according to the directions of Luis Buñuel
> reproducing the sound-track which he created
> for the first screening, using gramophone records.']

ii   Main title 1, white script on black background:

UN CHIEN ANDALOU

iii   Main title 2, same style:

Mise en scène
de Louis [*sic*] Buñuel
[English translation: 'Direction by Luis Buñuel']

iv   Main title 3, same style:

d'après un scénario
de Salvador Dali
et Louis [*sic*] Buñuel.

[English translation: 'From a scenario by Salvador Dali and Luis
Buñuel.']
Dissolve.

v   Main title 4, same style:

avec
Simonne [*sic*] Mareuil
et Pierre Batchef [*sic*].

[English translation: 'With Simone Mareuil and Pierre Batcheff.']
Dissolve.

vi   Main title 5, same style:

Prise de vues: Duverger.

[English translation: 'Cinematography: Duverger.']

Segment 1: Shots 1–13

1   First Inter-Title:

Il était une fois . . .

[English translation: 'Once Upon a Time . . .']

2   Fade-in. A man's bare arms and hands enter frame right, and
stroke a razor backwards and forwards on a strop attached to the
handle of a French window left. The camera is looking down, at an
obtuse angle to the window. The strop is at a right-angle to the
window.

3   Head-and-shoulders semi-frontal shot of a man in front of a
curtained window, cigarette in mouth, looking down and off-screen
right.

4   Similar to 2. Hand takes razor and tests it on thumb-nail.

5   Similar to 3.

6   Medium square shot of man left-profile against French windows. He examines the strop and razor, then opens doors to go outside.

7   Longer square shot of balcony on to which man has just emerged, seen from opposite. He looks around him, and out across the balcony, seeming to continue to test razor on thumb before stopping with hands on parapet.

8   Head-and-shoulders, three-quarter, right-profile of man as he raises head to look upwards.

9   Long shot of darkened sky with moon distant left, approached by slivers of horizontal cloud from right.

10   Similar to end of 8.

11   Square close-up of the female protagonist's face, other character's (man's) body half-glimpsed to her left (screen right), using left hand to open her left eye. When he does so, his right hand enters frame with razor and he goes to draw razor across eye. The man is now wearing a striped tie.

12   Similar to 9, but moon now sliced by cloud.

13   Close-up of eye, held open by fingers, slit by razor, exuding jelly.

Segment 2: Shots 14–24

14   Second Inter-Title:

Huit ans après.

[English translation: 'Eight Years Later.']

15   Fade-in. Long shot down city street left, from pavement. Corner of large building square opposite. Cyclist enters frame right, wearing cap, cape and apron over suit. He cycles down street left, on left-hand side, into distance.

16   Long shot of another street running left foreground to right distance. Cyclist appears right-centre, on right-hand side of street, travelling left. As he approaches frame left, dissolve.

17   Frontal shot of cyclist cycling down one side of another street,

now seen to be wearing a striped box hanging from a cord round his neck. The camera tracks back with him, panning slightly to keep him in frame.

18   Tracking shot forward down street, similar to shot 15.

19   Similar to shot 17, but camera lower, cutting head of cyclist, and showing handlebars.

20   Similar to 18. Dissolve.

21   Back-view of cyclist, cap, cape and skirt visible in super-imposition over street. Superimposition fades, leaving static back-view of cyclist against dark background. Dissolve.

22   Long-shot down city street, large building left, park right. The cyclist rides from foreground down street into distance. Dissolve remains as superimposition until cut.

23   Medium shot across street foreground to left distance, park-railings opposite. The cyclist wobbles across from left towards camera, camera panning slightly to frame him, and down to box as he approaches. Dissolve.

24   Close-up of diagonally striped box. Fade-out.

Segment 3: Shots 25–44

25   Fade-in. Square shot of bedsitting room. The female protagonist is seated at a table in centre foreground, reading, across the table from an empty chair. In the background are, left to right, a standard lamp, a single bed and chair, a curtained window and a further chair in the corner. There is a picture on the wall on each side of the window. Dissolve.

26   Frontal waist-shot of the female protagonist reading, left, door behind her, dresser and mirror behind her in right distance. She looks up and off to her left, screen right.

27   Square, frontal shot across street to building opposite. Cyclist enters frame left and exits frame right. The shot opens and closes with his entry to, and exit from, the frame.

28   Similar to end of 26. The female protagonist slams book shut, and throws it on to table. A mouse-cage visible behind the book, a

corkscrew-like object in front.

29 Close-up of book falling open on to table, revealing a left-hand page of print facing a right-hand full-page reproduction of Vermeer's 'The Lace-maker' centre frame.

30 Close shot of the female protagonist, the camera panning up and right as she rises and crosses room, exiting frame right on cut.

31 Medium shot of the female protagonist entering frame right. The camera pans left with her, stopping as she draws lace curtain to look through window, starting back.

32 Long shot down on to street running left foreground to right foreground. The diagonal is emphasized by shadow left, pavement right and angle of street-light. The camera pans slowly to follow cyclist from top of frame to middle.

33 Similar to 31. The female protagonist takes the lace once more, starting back in apparent anger.

34 Obliquely vertical long shot down onto street, frame divided diagonally – roadway left, pavement right. The cyclist, entering frame top right, rides to centre frame and topples off bicycle onto pavement.

35 The female protagonist turns in annoyance away from window, muttering to herself, then turns to move lace once more.

36 Vertical shot of fallen cyclist from position which diametrically reverses 34.

37 Similar to 35, the female protagonist muttering at window.

38 Square long shot of room, slightly closer than in 35. The female protagonist at window turns and walks defiantly towards bed.

39 Cut as the female protagonist reaches bed, camera panning left in mid-shot to follow her, stopping as she opens door and exits.

40 Close shot across prostrate cyclist, head on pavement behind.

41 Slightly left mid-shot of door at top of steps, which opens for the female protagonist to descend out of frame past camera right foreground.

42 Closer shot of cyclist, who has rolled over on to his back, the box having moved position to suit.

43   Slightly left mid-shot of doorway. The female protagonist exits, stands in doorway wringing hands, and then runs forward to stoop down bottom frame left.

44   Medium shot, slightly left, of cyclist, the female protagonist kneeling in gutter to hold his head in her hands as she kisses him numerous times. Doorstep visible in background. Dissolve.

Segment 4: Shots 45–61

45   Close-up of striped box being held in left hand against black background. Ringed and braceleted right hand enters frame left to unlock box, open it and remove diagonally striped packet.

46   Medium shot of the female protagonist standing at bedside. Holding packet in right hand, she puts box down with left hand, takes collar from bed, removes tie from collar, and unwraps diagonally striped tie to replace it on the bed. The camera wavers and pans slightly with her, stopping while she inserts new tie. She places new collar and tie on bed.

47   Medium close-up along bed of bib and apron, hands descending from top left to place collar and tie. The camera wavers to frame the shot, edge of box just visible bottom left. The camera tracks back along bed, wavering, to follow hands adjusting box and cyclist's skirt. Flash-frame effect.

48   Waist-shot across bed of the female protagonist sweeping foot of bed with right hand, looking over her work. The camera wavers and then pans left, right, as she comes round foot of bed to sit in chair which has been drawn up diagonal to bed. The tie is crossed.

49   Diagonal medium shot of bed. Collar and tie now open. Internal jump-cut as tie and collar magically close and knot.

50   Medium shot of the female protagonist in chair, seen in left-profile frontally from bed beside chair. She stares off-screen left.

51   As 49. Collar and tie now open. Internal dissolve as tie knots.

52   Head-and-shoulders shot of the female protagonist, three-quarters left-profile, looking left. She looks off-screen, right, and turns for a better look.

53 Medium shot of the male protagonist – who is the cyclist without frills – left-profile, left hand on hip, leaning forward to inspect right hand held up in front of face. Door left background, wall right.

54 Right forearm and palm run right bottom corner to top left of screen. Ants crawl in the palm around dark centre. The door is now visible left background.

55 As 53.

56 Mid-shot of the female protagonist, who has now turned in her chair right-profile to look off-screen right. A door is now visible behind her, right background. She rises.

57 Longer version of 53 and 55. The male protagonist's hand does not now overlap door. Lamp and drawers visible right. The female protagonist leaves chair left foreground – slightly turned, unexpectedly, to its right – to approach the male protagonist.

58 Medium shot of the male protagonist three-quarters right-profile left, the female protagonist three-quarters left-profile right. His hand and arm are now held at a different angle. Another door is now visible on far wall behind her.

59 Diagonal close-up of palm, crawling with ants which are emerging from a hole in the centre of the palm.

60 As 58. The female protagonist looks at the male protagonist's face. He turns his head to look at her. She looks back at his hand, as does he.

61 As 59. Dissolve.

Segment 5: Shots 62–63

62 Close-up of (woman's?) arm-pit, arm exiting frame left, head obscured by cap at top of frame, swimsuit right. Earth (sand?) just visible bottom left. Dissolve.

63 Vertical mid-shot of sea-urchin on sand centre-bottom frame, human footprint horizontal above it. Dissolve.

64   Darkened screen, apart from small patch of light centre top frame, revealing vertical overhead shot of figure poking cane at severed hand on ground. Other figures just visible in darkness round about.

65   Lower vertical shot. Figure and hand in iris just off-centre.

66   Similar to 65, but camera position as high as for 64. Iris opens to reveal a man struggling with a gendarme, and a crowd of onlookers.

67   Mid-shot, looking from lower angle, across heads of crowd to new woman in centre. She is unperturbed as two gendarmes attempt to disperse animated crowd.

68   Still closer waist-shot down on to new woman, lower torsos of crowd visible in background.

69   Close-up of severed hand on rough background. Cane touches its little finger, then the severed flesh at the wrist.

70   Medium shot of crowd, gendarme pulling back one man who moves across right to take a closer look.

71   As 68.

72   Medium shot of crowd, looking down left. Gendarme crosses frame right to left to restrain woman extreme left.

73   Low-angle waist-shot of woman and four men looking down left. Central male bystander anxiously rubs his wrist.

74   Medium shot looking down, woman's legs left, severed hand bottom right. Play of light and shadow represents motion of crowd.

75   Low-angle close shot of man, woman and two men looking over camera, buildings visible behind and above them in background.

76   Slightly low-angle medium shot of balcony and window, the male protagonist left, the female protagonist right, looking down right. He turns to her, apparently speaking, and then looks back down.

77   As 71.

78   As 76. The male protagonist stirs.

79   Medium shot down on new woman across foreground heads. Gendarme left foreground turns to new woman and salutes.

80   Waist-shot, gendarme right-profile left, new woman left-profile right. Looking towards her, he addresses her with some animus and then stoops.

81   Oblique vertical shot, frame ringed with heads of onlookers. One gendarme holds back crowd at top of frame. The other picks up the hand and goes to place it in the box – seemingly the same as the cyclist's – which he is holding in his left hand.

82   As 80. Gendarme places hand on box, closes lid, looks at new woman.

83   Head and shoulders shot of new woman, three-quarters left-profile, receiving box with some emotion, clutching it to her breast.

84   Closer waist-shot of couple at window. They look up and off in turn, moved.

85   As 83.

86   As 84. He looks up and away, then down left. She looks down ahead.

87   Oblique vertical shot. Ring of crowd surrounded by empty street, pavement diagonal left bottom, shadow top right. Gendarme salutes new woman with arm to breast. The gendarmes disperse crowd, who move off in all directions, casting strong shadows following diagonals of framing, leaving the new woman and her shadow alone in the centre of the screen, holding the box in front.

88   Long shot along street foreground to right background. The new woman stands front left foreground, clutching box to chest, looking away right and down. A car enters frame left directly behind her and travels towards distance.

89   Close shot of the male protagonist at the window, looking down intently left, biting lip.

90   As 88.

91   Interior close shot of couple at window. The female protagonist

right, back turned, the male protagonist left, right-profile, elbow resting on window-frame. He turns to her and speaks, gesturing with his face towards the window.

92 Similar to 87, but without shadow, only pavement visible left, new woman facing right bottom. Car enters bottom frame right. Couple on street cross top of frame, car passes directly behind new woman.

93 As 89.

94 As 92. Figure on pavement bottom left watches, then moves off, car passes new woman identically as in 92.

95 Waist-shot of new woman turning right-profile to look off right, pavement visible behind. Pedestrians cross behind and in front of her.

96 Square long shot down centre of street to watch car approaching from background. This does not appear to be the same street as in 88.

97 As 95. New woman catches sight of car.

98 Tracking shot from inside car, camera looking over bonnet-insignia at new woman ahead with hands in air, box on ground, as car bears down on her.

99 As 97, new woman cringing and clutching box.

100 Long shot along street from pavement. Roadway right foreground to left background. New woman left centre, box on ground again. Car enters bottom right corner to run her down.

101 As 93. The male protagonist is evidently excited.

102 As 92. New woman prostrate (that is, vertical in terms of screen surface) bottom frame right, as car travels to exit top left. One pair of feet pass on pavement top right. One man enters and goes to body from frame left, another from top right. Another comes in slowly from top right and a woman from bottom frame below body.

103 As 91. The male protagonist, impassioned, looks off to his right (screen left), and draws lace curtain.

104 Interior close view of couple at window, opposite to 91. Back

21

view of his right side left, her left-profile right. Although the end of 103 suggests he is now looking at her, he begins this shot still looking out of the window before turning his head to her.

Segment 7: Shots 105–158

105 Similar to 91. The male protagonist, left hand behind head, looking at the female protagonist right. He addresses her, gesturing with his look out of the window.

106 As 104. She looks up at him, speaks nervously, looks down again. He turns to her, and she looks back at him and pulls back.

107 As 105. The male protagonist, leaning forward, looks the female protagonist up and down.

108 Frontal mid-shot of window and wall right. The male protagonist, right-profile left, right hand on hip; the female protagonist right-profile centre right. He leans across, clutching her breasts; she pulls back and off-screen right, camera panning slightly as he follows.

109 Panning waist-shot of the male protagonist, three-quarters right-profile, as he looks off right, camera beginning to track back along long wall.

110 Tracking and wavering frontal waist-shot of the female protagonist as she retreats, looking off left.

111 Camera tracks back panning to follow the male protagonist in waist-shot, three-quarters right-profile, down long wall past door.

112 Camera tracks on the female protagonist as she moves back along wall, wavering slightly, as the male protagonist comes into frame left and moves round her to trap against wall beside table. He follows, and again jumps ahead of her, to trap her against the wall. Camera stops, then pans right, as he moves forward, with her retreating, to seize her breasts again.

113 Close shot of the female protagonist's torso, the breasts kneaded by the male protagonist's hands. She forces them away.

114 Waist-shot of the male protagonist, right-profile left, with the female protagonist left-profile centre right, fighting him off, then

staring angrily at him. He looks at her breasts, grins, and as her own look melts, begins to knead her breasts once more. She turns her head to the wall in seeming surrender.

115 Close shot of torso from the female protagonist's left-hand side. Dissolve.

116 As 115, but hands now kneading breasts on naked torso.

117 Low angle close-up of the male protagonist's head, the female protagonist's head partly visible bottom right corner of frame. His head is raised, his eyeballs rolled upwards; discoloured (bloody?) saliva is running to his chin from the right corner of his mouth.

118 As 116. Dissolve.

119 As 115.

120 Similar to 117, but at slightly different angle. The male protagonist's head is lowered. Drool drips from chin.

121 As 119. Dissolve.

122 Similar to 116, but hands now kneading buttocks on naked torso. Dissolve.

123 As 121.

124 Similar to 120, but at a slightly different angle. The male protagonist's face is now looking down at the female protagonist. He opens his mouth wide, purses his lips, and begins to smile. There is no sign of saliva.

125 As 114. The female protagonist looks off to her left, screen right, then angrily pushes the male protagonist out of frame left, and runs out of frame right.

126 Long shot down room. The male protagonist chases from right corner background round furniture in foreground as the female protagonist escapes into left corner background between the bed and wall.

127 Medium shot panning right as the female protagonist clambers across bed. Camera stops on view of window as she exits frame right, panning left again to pick up the male protagonist clambering across bed, panning right with him again to catch the female protagonist in

corner, defending herself with a chair.

128 Medium shot of the female protagonist in corner, looking down long wall to her left, grabbing tennis racquet with right hand from wall left and raising it above her head.

129 Long shot of the female protagonist in corner, right background, racquet raised, the male protagonist facing her with his back to camera in centre frame. He turns away, pauses, then turns back towards the female protagonist.

130 Head-and-shoulders shot of the male protagonist, tracking backwards, wavering.

131 As end of 128.

132 As 130, briefly, until the male protagonist and the camera stop.

133 Waist-shot version of 131, the female protagonist breathing heavily.

134 As 130. The male protagonist becoming uncertain and glancing off down left, off-screen right, then back at the female protagonist.

135 As 133.

136 Waist-shot version of 134. The male protagonist looks off left (screen right), feels in breast pocket, looks off right (screen left), looks backwards to his right, looks triumphantly forward, moves right and backwards, looks up once more in triumph, and stoops down out of frame, the camera panning down slightly as he does so.

137 Close shot down along carpeted floor. The male protagonist is on hands and knees, a rope in left hand. He feels about with right hand as though to find another, looking up as though to check the woman is still there.

138 As 135. The female protagonist gasps as though in horror.

139 Long shot across room. The female protagonist in corner, left. The male protagonist gets to his feet and pulls on ropes, bringing into view a pair of large, flat irregular rectangles attached to the ropes, but he is immediately braked and floored by the unexpected resistance of what he is pulling. He looks around and rises once

again, turning back to the female protagonist to make another effort, this time with the ropes over his shoulders. He glances back a couple of times between efforts to get moving.

140   Square medium shot across room, door partly visible left, table partly visible right. The male protagonist's head enters the frame right and he staggers across the frame, stumbling, bringing two large spherical objects briefly into view after the rectangles.

141   As 135. The female protagonist lowers her racquet, gasping as though in horror.

142   Continuation of 140. The male protagonist hardly progresses.

143   Long shot down room over keyboards and lids of two grand pianos, side by side, the lid of each propped open by a dead donkey with its head on the keyboard, seemingly attached to the ropes leading on to the male in the right background. Beyond the pianos the heads of two priests can just be made out, as though they are lying on the floor.

144   Close shot down on to a piano keyboard and the bloody head of a donkey that it bears, moving jerkily away from camera. The donkey's head appears to have an extra jaw-bone set in the side of its face. Blood is streaming from its damaged eye-socket.

145   As 143, the male protagonist looking back at his load. The female protagonist throws down her racquet.

146   As 141. The female protagonist cringes back against her left-hand wall. She turns to hide in corner.

147   As 142.

148   Close shot down on to two priests, supine on floor, hands folded across their midriffs, being apprehensively towed backwards.

149   High shot down on to the male protagonist as he struggles for a footing, and the priests, who appear to be helping the load along with their feet.

150   Head-and-shoulders shot of the female protagonist as she turns from the corner, only to give another gasp.

151   Similar to 144. Donkey's head in slightly different position.

152　As 148, but the right-hand priest of 148 is now seemingly replaced by his partner. The left-hand priest appears to be played by a new actor.

153　As 149.

154　As 145.

155　Medium shot across room, further left than in shot 142. The female protagonist is now visible in corner left. The male protagonist is wildly pulling, but only the rectangles are visible.

156　Close shot of the female protagonist, head and shoulders left. She darts a look left (screen right) and rapidly exits frame right.

157　Same camera position as in 155. The female protagonist is exiting through door. The male protagonist throws off the ropes to chase her. He runs into the wall left of door, and can only put his right hand through the door, which is closed on him.

158　Head-and-shoulders side view of the male protagonist in agony as his hand is trapped in the door.

Segment 8: Shots 159–173

159　Head-and-shoulders shot of the female protagonist pushing against the door left.

160　Longer version of 158, the male protagonist caught in the closed door vertical centre frame. His face goes through paroxysms of agony, and he throws his free right arm up and around his head as though to alleviate the pain.

161　Closer shot of the male protagonist left, head-and-shoulders in left lower quadrant of screen. His face remains extremely anguished as he repeats soothing movement with free hand and arm.

162　Similar to 159.

163　Waist-shot of the female protagonist at door, door-jamb vertical left with the male protagonist's outstretched hand coming through. Ants swarm in his palm as her eyes focus on it.

164　Closer shot of hand, clenching on itself. Ants swarm around a dark crater in its centre. Hand reopens, then begins to clench again.

165　As 163. Still struggling at the door, the female protagonist turns her gaze from the hand to look out of screen past camera right.

166　As 164. Hand clenches tightly upon itself.

167　As end of 165.

168　Shot of iron bedstead running left background to right foreground, curtained windows right. Lying straight out on the bed is the cyclist, hands at his side, wearing bonnet, bib and apron with a book lying across his chest. His diagonal is matched by a band of diagonal shadow falling parallel with him on the wall behind.

169　Close shot of the head on bed, staring up out of top of frame.

170　As end of 167. The female protagonist turns until her gaze is now directed left, off-screen right, as she moves away from the door.

171　As 169. The cyclist lowers his head bit by bit as he turns his gaze right, out of screen left, then in opposite direction, off-screen right, then back again as his mouth contorts into a smiling grimace, then back again.

172　As end of 170.

173　As 171, the cyclist looking off-screen left, screen right. He twice looks off in the opposite direction and back, his mouth opening in a grin or grimace of suppressed pleasure/anticipation.

Segment 9: Shots 174–211

174　Third Inter-Title:

Vers trois heures du matin . . .

[English translation: 'Towards Three in the Morning . . .']

175　Medium shot up stairway to door with balcony-rails on left. New male character gallops up stairs and presses bell right.

176　Close shot, as though from door, of arm crossing screen right to left to press bell left.

177　Frontal close shot of wooden panel, two circular holes cut out side by side to admit forearms which shake a cocktail-shaker.

178　As end of 173. The cyclist looks left (screen right).

179 As 177.

180 As end of 178. The cyclist looks apprehensive.

181 Waist-shot of the female protagonist, centre, left-profile, moving right away from door, speaking as though harshly. Camera pans right as she crosses room to door.

182 Medium shot, slightly left, up stairs to back of a newcomer and door. He swings his left arm impatiently until the door opens – revealing no one – whereupon he dashes inside and the door closes.

183 As 180.

184 Medium shot from behind the newcomer as he enters the bedroom door and strides over to the cyclist on the bed, waving his arm as though to tell the latter to get up.

185 Closer shot from behind the newcomer to the bed. He repeats the gesture, then leans forward to gesticulate with both hands. Dissolve.

186 Close shot looking down at the cyclist as though from the newcomer's point-of-view. The cyclist raises his head as though he cannot understand what he sees, then falls back on the bed with a grimace of fear.

187 Medium shot along bed. The newcomer's left side is visible right.

188 As 186. The cyclist cowers back.

189 As 187. The newcomer bends forward low over the cyclist and grabs for his neck.

190 New close shot of the cyclist's head, looking left off-screen as hands left secure a hold on his bib and tug at him. They shake him up and down, to his evident bafflement, and finish by jerking him out of the frame.

191 As 189. Brief shot of the newcomer jerking the cyclist out of bed towards him.

192 Long shot of the bedroom, slightly right. The newcomer pulls the cyclist away from the bed to stand up in centre frame. The newcomer thrusts himself forward at the cyclist, tears off his cap and

the other items, then goes over to the windows, and moves to open them with his left hand.

193   Medium shot, slightly right, of the windows, the newcomer left. He opens the windows with his right hand, then throws a piece of clothing out.

194   Low-angle long shot up to the windows, with the building as though sloping down right to left. Cut as a garment disappears from frame bottom left.

195   As end of 193. The newcomer throws out another object.

196   As 194. Again, cut as object leaves the frame.

197   As 195, except that it is as though the newcomer is still poised after throwing out the last item, or has just thrown out another.

198   Medium shot of the cyclist in front of bed. He discovers the cord still around his neck and hurriedly attempts to stuff it into his right pocket, screen left, to hide it.

199   Similar to 197, the newcomer closing window and turning left to look off-screen.

200   The cyclist is surprised, interrupted. He is already proffering what he has been attempting to hide as hands enter frame right to take it.

201   Medium shot past the newcomer to the cyclist opposite. The newcomer is evidently angry with cyclist.

202   Similar to 200. The cyclist right-profile left.

203   Head-and-shoulders close shot over the newcomer as he opens the window to hurl out cord.

204   Shorter low-angle shot of balcony. Shot cuts as item reaches bottom frame.

205   Medium shot, slightly right, of window right, bed left. The cyclist three-quarter right-profile left, the newcomer square back-view right as he walks backwards from window to point off-screen right with right arm. The cyclist shakes his head vigorously. The newcomer insists on his gesture. The cyclist reluctantly walks right, clasping hands behind back. The camera pans right to follow him

past the newcomer until he finally stands face against the wall right, between chair and door, beside a tennis racquet and cap hanging on the wall. The camera stops with him.

206 Waist-shot of the cyclist quarter right-profile against the wall. His shadow has thickened. He turns to look directly at the camera and frowns before resignedly turning back to the wall.

207 Waist-shot of the newcomer, back view, right, the cyclist background left, similar angle to 206. The newcomer throws up both arms, the cyclist turns and begins to do same.

208 Similar to end of 206. The cyclist turns from wall and puts hands up, turning back to wall.

209 Similar to 207. The newcomers back out of frame right.

210 Similar to end of 208.

211 Long shot along the room. The cyclist and newcomer in corner, left frame; the long wall runs empty left to right, although a chair has now appeared between the door and table right. The newcomer backs towards the camera. He throws hat off-screen left with left hand, backs again and begins to turn right, as though to reveal himself.

Segment 10: Shots 212–237

212 Fourth Inter-Title:

Seize ans avant.

[English translation: 'Sixteen Years Before.']

213 Similar to beginning of 211, except no chair now visible. The newcomer, now further down the room, turns towards the camera, in slow motion, film grainy. He advances towards the camera. He is the cyclist's double. His hands clutched imploringly before him, he looks off left over the camera and at the camera before opening his arms as he reaches the foreground.

214 Close shot down on to a school-desk running diagonally left foreground to right foreground. An exercise book, and a smaller book, are open on it, the latter covered with a blotter. There is also a pen and debris on the desk.

215   Longer version of 211, the desk in foreground left, the new-comer approaching it as though in a spirit of discovery.

216   Similar to 214. Hands bottom frame remove the blotter and close book to look at its title. The other exercise book is also closed, and both are removed from the frame.

217   Similar to 215. The newcomer holds the books in front of him, gazing at empty desk, before turning away from camera.

218   Jump-cut to very slightly advanced version of 217, from very slightly different camera position, as the newcomer walks back towards the cyclist in the corner, now in standard motion.

219   Similar to 208. The cyclist looks off-screen right.

220   Almost square medium shot of wall left, cyclist left frame, right-profile, door right, newcomer left-profile. The newcomer takes a step forward and proffers the book to the cyclist as the latter turns.

221   Similar to 219, but the cyclist holding out his hands right to receive books from hands entering the frame right. With a grin, he resumes his former position facing the wall, arms outstretched, giving a look off right.

222   Head-and-shoulders shot of the newcomer, three-quarters left-profile, shaking his head in wonder. Grainy slow motion.

223   Waist shot, grainy, of the newcomer, left-profile against door centre frame, reaching out, as though in pity, towards the cyclist partly visible frame left. He then turns away, shaking head in resigned wonder, to drift away right.

224   Medium shot of door right, the cyclist against wall left. He turns to face the camera, holding books as though they were guns.

225   Rear waist-shot of the newcomer approaching door opposite, past mirror right, in which is reflected a chair.

226   Similar to end of 224, books becoming revolvers via an internal jump-cut. The cyclist calls out.

227   Longer version of 225, in which the newcomer now appears further away from the wall. He stops and turns as he reaches door.

228   Shot over head and shoulders of the newcomer, shifting, to

cyclist with revolvers in far corner.

229   Similar to later part of 226. The cyclist speaks again.

230   Similar to 228. The newcomer raises his hands.

231   Grainy head-and-shoulders shot, slightly left, of the new-comer, still dreamily anxious.

232   Frontal waist-shot of the cyclist and his guns, frame left. He gestures the newcomer to put his hands up.

233   Similar to 231.

234   Similar to 232. The cyclist fires three times.

235   Similar to 228 as the cyclist fires three more times. In the foreground the newcomer begins to sag.

236   Similar to 233. The newcomer's eyes roll up, his hands clutch, sag.

237   Close-up, slightly right, of the gunman's middle as he fires twice more.

Segment 11: Shots 238–255

238   Continuation of 236. The newcomer's hands fall, his body convulses, sags.

239   Frontal head-and-shoulders shot of the newcomer against a background of trees as he falls forward past the camera. Cut as his head disappears out of frame.

240   Medium shot across a patch of grass to a tree-lined lake and land beyond. The newcomer falls into frame left, on to his knees, falling forward to clutch the back of a naked woman, also kneeling forward. Her back is turned; she is wearing a pearl necklace; a cloak or dress is drawn around her buttocks.

241   Waist-shot of the woman's back, quarter right-profile. The newcomer's face and hands are partly visible frame left, his right hand slipping off woman's shoulder and out of frame bottom.

242   Continuation of 240. The newcomer falls prostrate across the bottom of the frame. The woman dissolves out of the image.

243   Long shot of the body in parkland. Two male figures hurry forward extreme left background. A male figure enters frame right, crosses to body, as does another male figure from frame left, and further single male figures from bottom frame right and bottom frame left.

244   Longish shot past bush right foreground to two male strollers advancing left towards the camera.

245   Medium shot of four figures at body. Two kneeling men roll the body over and inspect the jacket. The left figure is despatched out of frame left; one listens for a heartbeat.

246   Similar to end of 244. Strollers walk into waist-shot.

247   Similar to end of 245.

248   Long shot of empty grass through overhead boughs, trees in distance. Two strollers walk from just inside frame left, right, camera panning right to follow as a man appears bottom frame left to accost them. The camera stops as he reaches them mid-screen.

249   Reverse medium shot of the accoster, left, couple right. They cross left, apparently ignoring his appeal.

250   Continuation of 248. The camera pans slightly right as they separate, so that the accoster and the strollers exit bottom frame left, bottom frame right, simultaneously.

251   Long shot of three figures at the body. Messenger runs into frame left, gesturing off-screen left. Strollers unexpectedly enter screen left as one kneeler rises. Taller stroller gives wave of indifferent approval and moves round to the right of the group, looking off. His companion exits frame left, leading four figures bearing body. As they leave frame left, he turns to follow them. Cut after he crosses frame and exits left.

252   Frontal long shot of the cortège approaching camera down woodland.

253   Frontal medium shot of the cortège, camera tracking back.

254   Continuation of 251. As leader exits bottom frame left, dissolve.

255   Long shot down on to rear of cortège. Fade.

256   Fade-in. Leftish medium shot of door, drawers right, mirror visible. Right, reflection of bed in mirror. Door opens, female protagonist enters, looking left (screen right). Dissolve.

257   Frontal waist-shot of the female protagonist closing the door behind her, now looking right (screen left).

258   Medium shot of empty wall, a moth visible near its centre, shadow above. The light expands as though in a diffuse iris. Dissolve.

259   Close shot of fully lit empty frame, moth now larger near centre bottom.

260   Similar to end of 257.

261   Similar to 259. Dissolve.

262   Close-up, moth now identifiable as a death's head moth, filling screen with wing-span. Iris-in to body and skull.

263   Extreme close-up of skull on moth.

264   Head-and-shoulders shot of the female protagonist looking left (screen right), fierce. She starts forward.

265   Similar to 263.

266   Grainy waist-shot of the male protagonist, three-quarters left-profile left, looking across shadowed screen right.

267   Similar to 257, the female protagonist against door.

268   Similar to 266. The male protagonist suddenly claps hand to mouth.

269   Similar to 264. The female protagonist looks puzzled, 'tuts' in anger.

270   Nearly frontal waist-shot of the male protagonist in centre screen, surrounded by shadow, looking left (screen right). He wipes his hand across his mouth to reveal that his mouth has vanished, and drops his hand to his side.

271   Similar to 267, the female protagonist calling defiantly and producing a lipstick and mirror to colour in her own mouth.

272   Waist-shot of the male protagonist, three-quarters left-profile, looking off right (screen left). A dark patch dissolves in over his missing mouth.

273   Similar to end of 271. The female protagonist drops her cosmetics, throws out her arms in horror and throws up her right arm to examine it with her left hand.

274   Close shot of the female protagonist's arm and breast confirms the hair has vanished from her armpit.

275   Long shot over the male protagonist's head, right foreground to the female protagonist, left background. The bed appears to have changed position, and the table set-up is unclear. She gestures angrily and grabs for something out of frame left.

276   Medium shot of the female protagonist grabbing and putting on scarf.

277   Similar to end of 272.

278   Head-and-shoulders shot of the female protagonist sticking out her tongue, looking off left (screen right), tossing up her head in defiance and exiting through door, which she closes after her.

279   Similar to 275, minus the female protagonist.

280   Similar to 278, the female protagonist jeering through a gap in the door bottom frame.

Segment 13: Shots 281–294

281   Medium shot of the female protagonist, centre, closing door left, wall at another angle right. A wind is blowing, and she turns to face camera, looking past it right.

282   Long shot over shallow band of shingle to sea. Back-view of a man, hands on hips, in right foreground. A sail is visible on the horizon. He turns to look off left, screen right.

283   Similar to end of 281. The female protagonist waves, exits right bottom frame.

284   Medium shot of new man turning to look off right and slightly left.

285   Long shot along water's edge, the resort curving along horizon. New man frontal left foreground. The female protagonist enters right foreground and runs forward to hug his shoulder. He looks off right (screen left) as she does so.

286   Frontal waist-shot of new man looking off right (screen left), the female protagonist hanging on his shoulder, imploringly. Without looking at her, he holds up to her face the watch on his right wrist.

287   Close-up of the female protagonist's face, right-profile, left, man's fist and wrist, right. Angle does not correlate with 286, nor does background building. She looks up at him off right, pulls down his hand with her own, smiles, exits frame right.

288   Similar to beginning of 286, the female protagonist kissing face of unmoved new man. She forces his face round to look at her. The keel of a vessel crosses top of frame left to right. He flings down what he is holding in right hand, throws his arms round her, and embraces her. Dissolve.

289   Long shot along water-line in the opposite direction. The couple march off happily entwined, the camera panning slightly right as they follow the water's edge.

290   Reverse long-shot across rocky shingle to horizon. The couple walk along the waterline from frame left to centre foreground.

291   Medium shot down on to wet, rocky shore, containing remnants of cyclist's costume. The couple's legs enter frame left background and advance to remnants.

292   Close shot down on to feet and remnants. The new man budges box with foot. He kicks some of it off-screen right, then the remainder.

293   Similar to end of 291. The female protagonist bends down into frame to pick up soggy clothing. The camera pans up with her to stop as she smilingly presents them to the new man in medium shot. He throws four items one by one out of frame bottom left. They clamber arm in arm towards the camera and disappear foreground right.

294   Long shot along beach towards empty horizon, the camera

wavering right to follow the couple, who embrace. The headline 'Au printemps . . .' [English translation: 'In the Spring . . .'] dissolves in over the shot, which fades, leaving the lettering on the black screen for some time as an inter-title. Dissolve.

Segment 14: Shot 295

295   A still image of a desert-style landscape in medium shot. The female protagonist, and a male figure whom the scenario intends to be the male protagonist but who is difficult to identify in the shot, are buried up to their waists in the left and right foreground respectively. She is looking up, he is looking down. The scenario tells us that they have been blinded, but this is difficult to decipher in the image. Large winged insects can be seen around their bodies. The lettering fades, leaving just the image of the couple. Fade.

End title.

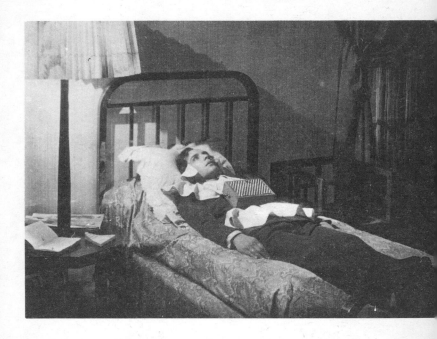